ORGAN TRANSPLANTS

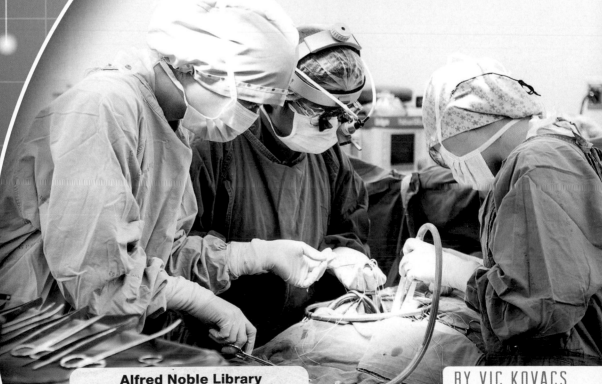

BY VIC KOVACS

Gareth Stevens
PUBLISHING

Please visit our website, www.garethstevens.com.
For a free color catalog of all our high-quality books, call toll free 1-800-542-2595 or fax 1-877-542-2596.

Cataloging-in-Publication Data

Names: Kovacs, Vic.
Title: Organ transplants / Vic Kovacs.
Description: New York : Gareth Stevens Publishing, 2017. | Series: Miracles of medicine | Includes index.
Identifiers: ISBN 9781482461008 (pbk.) | ISBN 9781482461701 (library bound) | ISBN 9781482461015 (6 pack)
Subjects: LCSH: Transplantation of organs, tissues, etc.--Juvenile literature.
Classification: LCC RD120.76 K68 2017 | DDC 617.9'5--dc23

Published in 2017 by
Gareth Stevens Publishing
111 East 14th Street, Suite 349
New York, NY 10003

Copyright © 2017 Gareth Stevens Publishing

Developed and produced for Rosen by BlueApple*Works* Inc.

Managing Editor for BlueApple*Works*: Melissa McClellan
Designer: Joshua Avramson
Photo Research: Jane Reid
Editor: Marcia Abramson

Photo Credits: Cover Johnny Greig/Getty Images; title page Tim Hipps, FMWRC Public Affairs/ The U.S. Army/Public Domain; title page background Wutthichaic/Shutterstock; p. 6 William Holl/Public Domain; p. 7 Sescoi CAD/CAM/Creative Commons; p. 9 Tatjana Kabanova/Shutterstock; p. 10 joyfull/Shutterstock; p. 11 wavebreakmedia/Shutterstock; p. 13 Helga Esteb/Shutterstock.com; p. 14 TFoxFoto / Shutterstock.com; p. 15 Helga Esteb/Shutterstock.com; p. 18 Susan Marie Sullivan/Shutterstock; p. 19 DGLimages/Shutterstock; p. 21, 26, 33, 35 belushi/Shutterstock; p. 22 Ericsmandes/Shutterstock; p. 23 sportpoint/Shutterstock.com; p. 25 Sgt. 1st Class Michael R. Noggle, USASOC Public Affairs/ The U.S. Army/Public Domain; p. 27 Defense Advanced Research Projects Agency (DARPA)/DOD/Public Domain; p. 28, 31 Photo Courtesy of U.S. Army/Public Domain; p. 29 Petty Officer 2nd Class Greg Mitchell of the United States Navy/U.S. Navy/Public Domain; p. 34 ChooChin/Shutterstock; p. 37 Lorena Fernandez/Shutterstock; p. 39 Rena Schild/Shutterstock.com; p. 41 TTStock/Shutterstock.com

Printed in the United States of America
CPSIA compliance information: Batch CW17GS: For further information contact Gareth Stevens, New York, New York at 1-800-542-2595.

CONTENTS

Chapter 1
The History of Organ Transplants 4

Chapter 2
The Organs 10

Chapter 3
Organ Donations 20

Chapter 4
The Transplant Process 28

Chapter 5
Improving Survival 34

Chapter 6
The Future of Transplant Surgery 40

Timeline of Organ Transplant Developments 44

Glossary 46

For More Information 47

Index 48

CHAPTER 1

THE HISTORY OF ORGAN TRANSPLANTS

The 20th century was an incredible period for medicine. From the discovery of antibiotics, to the widespread adoption and use of vaccines, science was constantly introducing new innovations that saved thousands of lives. One of the most miraculous developments during this time was a series of breakthroughs that led to organ transplants becoming a common and reliably successful procedure.

Although successful organ transplants only became commonplace during the 20th century, their beginnings stretch far back into human history. As early as 800 BC, doctors in India were performing the first skin grafts. These early procedures involved taking skin from the forehead and using it to construct a new nose for criminals who had theirs cut off as punishment.

FIRST STEPS

GASPARE TAGLIACOZZI TAUGHT AND PRACTICED **SURGERY** IN BOLOGNA, ITALY, DURING THE OFTEN WAR-TORN AND VIOLENT 16TH CENTURY. HE DEVELOPED RECONSTRUCTION TECHNIQUES TO HELP PATIENTS WHO HAD LOST A NOSE, A LIP, OR AN EAR WHILE FIGHTING WITH SWORDS OR KNIVES. TODAY TAGLIACOZZI IS CONSIDERED THE FOUNDER OF PLASTIC SURGERY.

IDENTIFYING BLOOD TYPES

Human beings each possess one of four different blood types. The first three, A, B, and O, were discovered by an Austrian doctor named Karl Landsteiner (1868–1943) in 1901. The fourth, AB, was found by scientists working under him the next year.

Blood types are classified based on the different types of **antigens** and **antibodies** they possess. Because foreign antigens provoke a response from the body's immune system, it's important that **transfusion** patients are given compatible blood. Type A blood has the A antigen and B antibody, Type B has the B antigen and A antibody, AB has both antigens but neither of the antibodies, and O has neither antigen but both antibodies. This discovery was a major breakthrough in understanding why some organ transplants were successful while others failed.

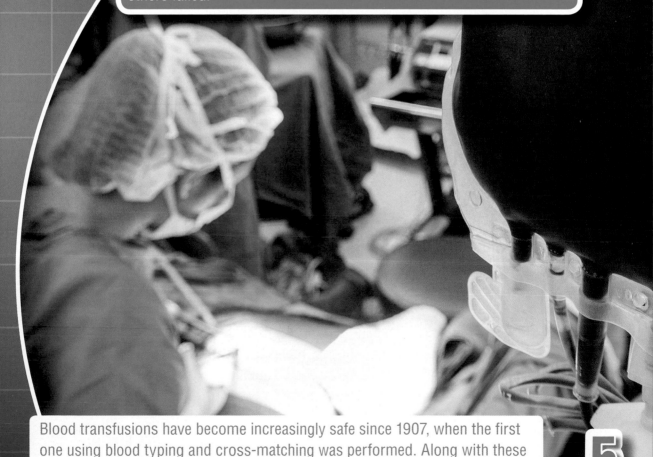

Blood transfusions have become increasingly safe since 1907, when the first one using blood typing and cross-matching was performed. Along with these safeguards, transfusions must be prescribed by a doctor.

The *Liezi*, a Chinese philosophical text from around 400 BC, seems to describe the first organ transplant between two patients. It contains a legend that claims Bian Que, the first known doctor in Chinese history, once switched the hearts of two men in an attempt to make them well again. Although this story almost certainly didn't happen, it shows that the idea of transplanting organs has been around for thousands of years.

Gaspare Tagliacozzi was an Italian surgeon who lived near the end of the 16th century. He came up with a technique that used skin from the arm to build a new nose. In doing so, he realized something that Indian doctors had discovered almost 2,000 years ago: The skin could only stay alive if blood kept flowing through it. As a result, his technique forced patients to keep their arm connected to their new nose until it grew a new blood supply. Imagine having to walk around for weeks looking like you were about to sneeze before your nose could be detached from your arm! Through this technique he also discovered something that would have far-reaching effects for transplant science.

Gaspare Tagliacozzi (1545–1599) gave illustrated instructions for rebuilding noses in a book published in 1597. Even so, his technique fell out of use in the 17th century and was forgotten until its rediscovery in 1800.

Tagliacozzi discovered that he could only transplant skin from the patient's own body, and not from another patient. Today we know that foreign tissue is rejected by the body's immune system, but this wasn't discovered until long after Tagliacozzi's time.

There were many hurdles that needed to be overcome before organ transplants could be done successfully. Dr. James Blundell performed the first successful blood transfusion in 1818. He managed to save a woman who was losing a lot of blood after giving birth by giving her blood provided by her husband. Although she survived, Blundell had trouble replicating his results. However, discovering that blood transfusions were possible was an important development. Before this discovery, a serious wound was usually deadly because it was impossible to replace lost blood.

Antiseptics to fight germs and anesthetics to control pain were also hugely important surgical innovations. Before anesthesia, patients were subjected to incredible pain during surgery. Once surgeons began using ether, surgeries that would have once been unendurable became possible.

7

Antiseptics also drastically reduced surgery-related deaths. Before surgeons used antiseptics, even if a surgery was successful, there was still a high chance the patient would die from infection in their surgical wounds. Using chemicals such as bleach or carbolic acid to sterilize both the surgical room and instruments made procedures much safer.

Transplant science really began to take off at the beginning of the 20th century. In 1902, Emerich Ullman, a surgeon from Hungary, transplanted a kidney from one dog into the neck of another. The kidney continued to work for five days. In 1909, a girl in France suffering from kidney failure was given transplanted slices of rabbit kidney. Although the surgery seemed successful at first, the girl died after two weeks.

In 1933, Yurii Voronoy of Ukraine attempted the first human-to-human kidney transplant using a kidney from a donor who had died. The transplant patient did not survive because her body rejected the new organ. This failure helped scientists realize that organ rejection was the primary problem they needed to solve.

The first successful kidney transplant took place in 1954. Richard Herrick received a kidney from his twin brother Ronald. This led to a key breakthrough: organs transplanted from one identical twin to another were not rejected. Knowing this, scientists came to understand that the patients' immune systems were recognizing foreign antigens present in the new organs and attacking them. This led to two innovations that helped lead to successful organ transplants. The first was suppressing the immune system so it wouldn't attack the new organ. This is now called **immunosuppression**. The second was matching donors to patients with similar **biological** traits.

Surgeons were performing more and more successful organ transplants as a result of these innovations, but one type remained elusive: a human-to-human heart transplant. This changed in 1967 when Dr. Christiaan Barnard performed the first successful operation of this kind. Though the recipient only survived for 18 days, the surgery proved that heart transplants were possible.

Surgeons worldwide were hesitant to perform a heart transplant until Dr. Christiaan Barnard (1922–2001) of South Africa led the way. He also helped to pioneer heart-lung transplants.

CHAPTER 2
THE ORGANS

Amazing advances have been made in the last hundred years in the field of organ transplantation. But what exactly are organs, and why do they sometimes need to be transplanted? An organ is a collection of tissues within the body that have evolved into a particular structure to perform a specific function. Often, individual organs, when taken together, form a larger organ system. For example, the stomach and several other organs together form the digestive system. Sometimes, for a variety of reasons, an organ can stop working. This can cause serious health problems. When one organ stops working properly, it also can have adverse affects on other organs. Depending on how badly the organ is damaged, and if that damage is reversible, the best option for treatment might be replacing the damaged organ with a healthier one. This is called an organ transplant.

Despite the progress that has been made in the field, not all organs can be transplanted. One major example is the brain.

HARD WORKER
THE AVERAGE HUMAN HEART BEATS ABOUT 100,000 TIMES A DAY, AND PUMPS 2,000 GALLONS OF BLOOD!

MATCHING DONORS TO RECIPIENTS

There are always more people who need transplants than there are available organs. Someone has to decide who will get these organs. In the United States, the United Network for Organ Sharing (UNOS), a nonprofit organization in Richmond, Virginia, determines which patients will receive organs. This organization also runs the Organ Procurement and Transplantation Network (OPTN). UNOS maintains a database of patients who need organs and ranks them according to how ill they are and how much benefit they will get from a transplant. When an organ becomes available, UNOS identifies the best matches from this list.

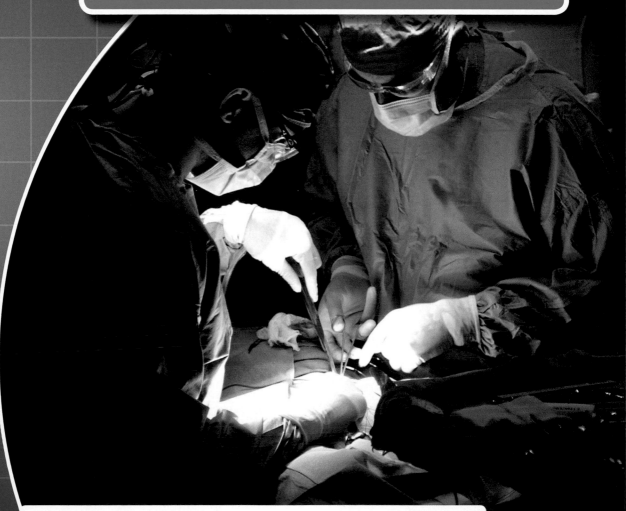

Kidney transplants have become the most common organ transplants. More than 17,000 were performed in 2014 in the United States.

Today, the majority of organ transplants involve the heart, kidneys, liver, lungs, intestine, or pancreas. Receiving just a single organ transplant is a major surgery, but recent advances have made it possible for some patients to get multiple transplants as part of the same procedure.

THE HEART

The heart is a muscular organ that is the driving force behind the body's circulatory system. About the size of a fist, it is located in the chest. The heart is made up of four separate chambers. The top chambers are called atria, and the lower chambers are called ventricles. The heart is usually divided into halves, with the right atrium and ventricle on the right half, and the left atrium and ventricle on the left half.

The heart's main function is to pump blood throughout the body. Blood delivers oxygen and **nutrients** to every part of the body, and it also picks up waste products, such as carbon dioxide, that the body produces. Deoxygenated blood is delivered to the right atrium, which pumps it to the right ventricle, which then pumps it to the lungs.

Each year, more than 4,000 patients receive new, healthy hearts.

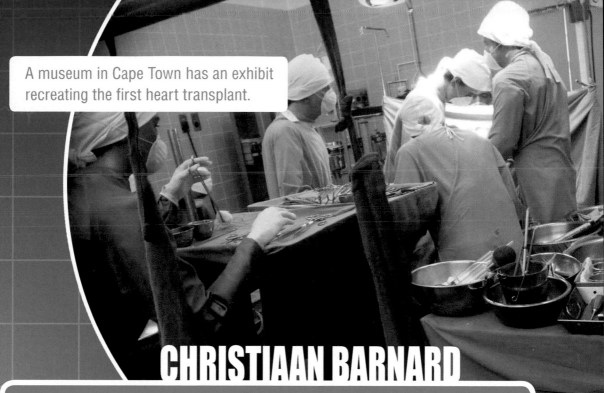

A museum in Cape Town has an exhibit recreating the first heart transplant.

CHRISTIAAN BARNARD

Christiaan Barnard was born in South Africa in 1922, the son of a preacher. He studied medicine at the University of Cape Town, and received his Ph.D abroad at the University of Minnesota. Upon returning home to South Africa, he introduced the country to open-heart surgery.

A talented surgeon, Barnard performed many experimental heart transplants on dogs. By 1967, he felt ready to attempt the first ever heart transplant on a human being. Louis Washkansky suffered from diabetes and an incurable heart disease. He was willing to undergo the experimental operation because he understood that, even though it was risky, he would definitely die without it. The donor heart came from Denise Darvall, a woman who had become brain dead as a result of a traffic accident. The operation was a success, although this success was short-lived. The transplant worked and the heart continued to function. However, Washkansky caught pneumonia because he was taking drugs to suppress his immune system so that it wouldn't reject the heart. He only lived for 18 days after the operation. Barnard, though, became famous overnight for his revolutionary surgery. He continued to refine the procedure, and many of his later patients went on to live for years. He died in 2001, at the age of 78.

In the lungs, blood exchanges carbon dioxide for oxygen. It then flows to the left atrium of the heart, which pumps it to the left ventricle, which then pumps it to the rest of the body so it can deliver oxygen. Blood flows through a system of tubes called blood vessels. Arteries are blood vessels that carry oxygenated blood away from the heart to the rest of the body. Veins carry deoxygenated blood back to the heart. Capillaries are tiny blood vessels. Oxygen, carbon dioxide, and nutrients can pass right through capillaries' walls.

THE LUNGS

The lungs are a pair of organs located in the chest. They are the central part of the human respiratory system. People have a right lung and a left lung, one on either side of the heart. The right is the larger of the two. This is because the left lung shares its space with the heart, so it needs to be smaller.

The lungs are responsible for supplying the body with oxygen. Air that is rich in oxygen is drawn into the body through the mouth and nose. It travels down the trachea, or windpipe, to the two bronchi, which are airways that each supply one of the lungs. The bronchi then divide into tinier pathways called bronchioles, which are connected to alveoli, tiny bags filled with air. Alveoli are surrounded by capillaries, which are filled with deoxygenated blood. The blood then trades its carbon dioxide for oxygen.

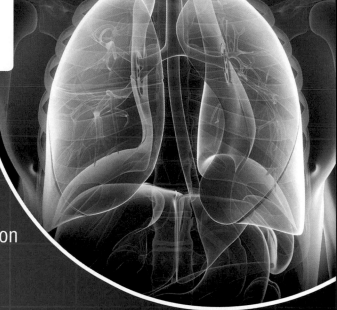

When a disease such as cystic fibrosis badly damages the lungs, a transplant may be a good option.

The oxygenated blood is then taken back to the heart, where it's pumped to the rest of the body, while the now carbon dioxide-rich air is expelled back the way it came.

KIDNEYS

The kidneys are two bean-shaped organs located in the lower back, just past where the rib cage ends, on either side of the spine. Like the heart, they're each about the size of a fist. They're part of the body's renal system and they perform many important functions, such as producing hormones that help make red blood cells and maintain regular blood pressure. However, their best-known function is waste management. Kidneys filter waste products from blood, as well as excess water. These products are then sent to the bladder, where they are evacuated from the body as urine. This filtration is done by small constructions called nephrons. Nephrons are so small that an average adult kidney contains one million of them.

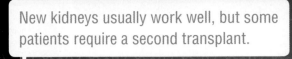
New kidneys usually work well, but some patients require a second transplant.

This filtration is a very important bodily function. If a kidney becomes damaged, or unable to perform its job, waste can build up inside the human body, essentially causing it to become poisoned from within. One way to deal with this is a process called **dialysis**, in which blood is removed, filtered externally, and returned to the body. However, in severe cases a kidney transplant might be the best treatment option. Common causes of kidney disease include diabetes and high blood pressure.

THE INTESTINES

Human beings have two different intestines: the small intestine and the large intestine. The small intestine is much narrower and much longer than the large intestine. Together, they form an integral part of the digestive system. Food that has been partially digested and broken down enters the small intestine from the stomach. There, it mixes with bile and pancreatic fluid to further break it down. Then, nutrients are absorbed from the food into the bloodstream. Once all the nutrients have been absorbed, the broken-down food is turned into fecal matter.

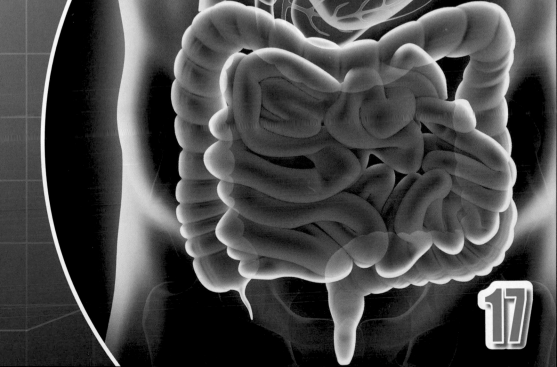

This fecal matter then enters the large intestine, where water is removed and absorbed from the feces. The large intestine then continues to move this matter along until it is expelled from the body as waste.

Currently, only the small intestine can be transplanted. This is also known as a small bowel transplant. It is usually done only as a last resort, when the patient's small intestine is no longer able to absorb nutrients. It is the least common kind of organ transplant, though it has become more common in recent years.

Intestinal transplants often include the liver as well, and may also include the stomach and pancreas. The difficulty of this complex surgery increases with each diseased organ that must be replaced.

THE LIVER

The liver is the largest internal organ in the human body, and the second largest overall. Only the skin eclipses it in terms of size. Located in the middle of the torso, it sits just under the heart and just above the stomach. The liver is responsible for many essential functions for a healthy body. It produces bile, which is exported to the small intestine and aids in digestion. It is where glucose, a kind of sugar, is stored and released as the body needs it. It also acts as a filter, cleansing blood of things like drugs and alcohol, which it breaks down into forms the body can more easily deal with. On top of these important jobs, it performs many other functions.

Because the liver is responsible for so much, it is important that it remains functional. If it doesn't, it can lead to many issues that can also affect other organs. A few common liver problems include hepatitis, which is when the liver becomes inflamed; cirrhosis, when it becomes scarred, and hepatic encephalopathy, which is when toxins that are normally filtered out of the blood by the liver build up instead. Alcohol abuse is also a major cause of liver damage.

Liver transplants have a good success rate, and more than 6,000 are performed each year in the United States.

THE PANCREAS

The pancreas is an organ located in the **abdomen**, just behind the stomach. It has a few major functions, including manufacturing pancreatic juices that help break down food and absorb nutrients in the small intestine. It also makes several important hormones, including insulin. Insulin allows glucose in the blood to be absorbed into other tissues in the body. Without it, the body cannot maintain proper blood sugar levels. This leads to other organs having trouble functioning, including the liver, kidneys, and brain.

The pancreas might have trouble producing insulin for a variety of reasons. This is called diabetes. Some types of diabetes can be regulated with regular injections of insulin, but others might be best treated with a pancreas transplant. There is also a procedure where pancreatic cells that produce insulin are transplanted into the liver. Once in place, they're able to produce insulin for the body again in their new home.

CHAPTER 3
ORGAN DONATIONS

An organ donor is someone who allows their organs to be removed and transplanted into someone else to improve the recipient's health. There are both living donors and deceased donors. Each type has different procedures that need to happen before an organ can be donated. These procedures are in place to ensure the safety and viability of both the donor and the receiver. Without donors, organ transplants would be impossible.

LIVING DONORS

Some organs, or parts of organs, can be donated from a living person. The most common organ donated by a living donor is the kidney. Humans can survive with very few issues with just one kidney. In fact, the remaining kidney will grow larger to make up for the loss of its partner. A whole lung can be donated, as well as just part of a lung.

TIME MATTERS

DIFFERENT ORGANS REMAIN **VIABLE** OUTSIDE THE BODY FOR DIFFERENT LENGTHS OF TIME. KIDNEYS CAN LAST FOR UP TO 48 HOURS, WHILE LIVERS CAN SURVIVE FOR EIGHT TO 20 HOURS. HEARTS AND LUNGS NEED TO BE USED MUCH MORE QUICKLY. THEY CAN ONLY LAST FOR A MAXIMUM OF SIX HOURS BEFORE THEY ARE NO LONGER USABLE.

Some organs are donated by people who just want to help others. These donors do not have a previous personal relationship with the recipient. They may hear about someone who needs an organ from friends or family, or in the news, or they may donate to the first compatible person on the UNOS list. These donors are often called good Samaritans, after the biblical story about helping a stranger. They may also be called altruistic unrelated donors or humanitarian donors. In 2013, there were about 6,000 such donors in the United States. Sometimes the donor and recipient agree to meet afterwards. Some even become close friends and fellow advocates for good Samaritan organ donation. These advocates tell their personal stories with the hopes of convincing others to become living donors.

Each year, thousands of people worldwide pass the physical and psychological screening tests to become living organ donors.

A living donor can also donate a lobe of liver, part of the pancreas, and part of the small intestine. In all of these cases, the donor retains almost full functionality of the partially donated organ, with no noticeable effects.

There are a few different types of living organ donors, and they each have different reasons for donating. Related donors are in the same family as the person who needs a donation. Because blood relatives often have the same blood and tissue types, a relative is often a good match with the person who needs an organ. The closer the match, the less likely the recipient's body is to reject the new organ. There are also unrelated donors who have close relationships with the recipients, even though they are not family. They might be a friend, or a godparent. There are also unrelated anonymous donors. An anonymous donor has no pre-existing relationship with the recipient, but simply wants to do a good thing for a stranger.

Whatever category living donors fall into, they are subject to a rigorous screening process. These tests are both physical and psychological.

The United States and many other countries allow directed donation, which means families can choose who gets a loved one's organs.

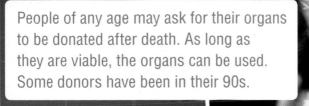

People of any age may ask for their organs to be donated after death. As long as they are viable, the organs can be used. Some donors have been in their 90s.

The physical tests determine if the donor is a suitable match and if they are in good enough health to donate. The psychological tests make sure that the donor will be able to handle the stress of the operation and the recovery process. They also make sure that the donor is donating their organ willingly, and not being forced to do so.

DECEASED DONORS

The majority of transplanted organs come from donors who have died. Deceased donors usually indicate their willingness to donate before they die. They might do this by registering with a state agency that keeps a database, or they might tell their doctor or paramedic before they pass. There are many causes of death that, while fatal, leave the victim with perfectly healthy organs. One common example is head trauma.

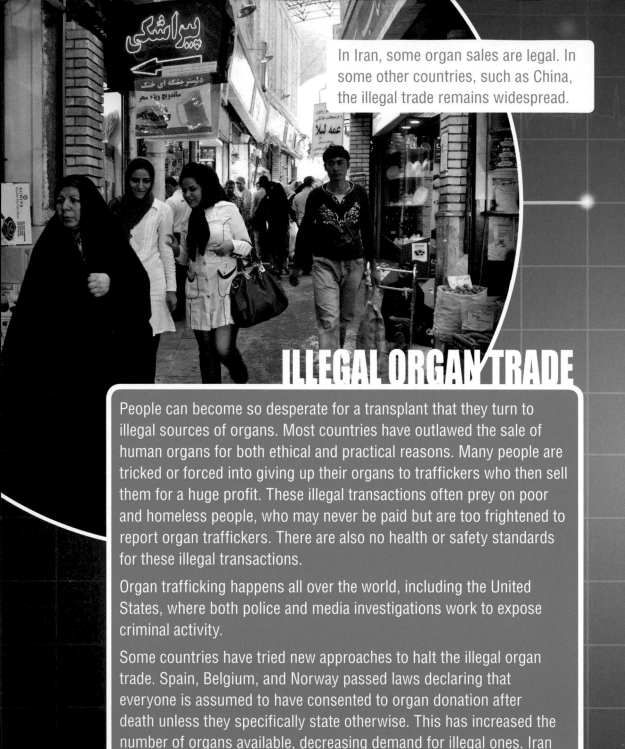

In Iran, some organ sales are legal. In some other countries, such as China, the illegal trade remains widespread.

ILLEGAL ORGAN TRADE

People can become so desperate for a transplant that they turn to illegal sources of organs. Most countries have outlawed the sale of human organs for both ethical and practical reasons. Many people are tricked or forced into giving up their organs to traffickers who then sell them for a huge profit. These illegal transactions often prey on poor and homeless people, who may never be paid but are too frightened to report organ traffickers. There are also no health or safety standards for these illegal transactions.

Organ trafficking happens all over the world, including the United States, where both police and media investigations work to expose criminal activity.

Some countries have tried new approaches to halt the illegal organ trade. Spain, Belgium, and Norway passed laws declaring that everyone is assumed to have consented to organ donation after death unless they specifically state otherwise. This has increased the number of organs available, decreasing demand for illegal ones. Iran has legalized payments for kidneys through a government-sanctioned program which has nearly eliminated its waiting list. Even so, these approaches raise ethical questions for many.

In some cases, organs are taken from patients whose brains no longer show any signs of activity, although their bodies may still be functioning on some level. Patients who are in this state are referred to as brain dead. There are strict guidelines in place to make sure that only patients who show no signs of brain activity or possible recovery are considered for potential donations. These tests are usually performed by a neurologist, or brain doctor, who had no part in the patient's earlier treatment, and who won't be involved in the transplant procedure. This is done so that they are impartial towards both the potential donor and the patient getting the organs.

One particular test is an electroencephalogram, or EEG. An EEG will tell doctors if there is any electrical activity in the brain. If there isn't, the brain is no longer able to perform even its most basic functions. Organs and tissues taken from just a single donor can help over 10 people. Sometimes a brain dead patient will have their body kept alive through artificial means to ensure the organs stay healthy until they can be harvested. Deceased donors are also the only source for important organs such as the heart, whole livers, and sets of lungs.

Most organ recipients in the United States are over 50 years old. In 2014, they made up 62 percent of all transplant recipients, according to statistics from UNOS. To date, most donor organs have come from deceased donors.

BEING A DONOR

Becoming an organ donor is a process that varies based on a few factors. The main determining factor is location. Different countries have different processes and regulations. Even within a single country, there might be different ways of registering. For example, in the United States, each state has different laws and processes. People often register as part of getting their driver's licenses in the United States.

In Canada, when people register to give blood they are asked if they'd also like to become an organ donor. If they are interested, they can decide which organs they'd like to donate. In England, people can receive a donor card, but it should be kept on them at all times. If it's not, doctors might not realize they're a donor.

Anyone wishing to be an organ donor should discuss their wishes with their family, though. Family members are often consulted about organ donation immediately after a loved one dies, and if the person's wishes aren't known, it can be a difficult decision to make in the heat of the moment.

Becoming a living donor involves a completely different and very thorough process. It generally takes a set amount of time during which many different tests are performed. Becoming a living donor is a very serious decision, and people who are considering it should discuss the matter with their doctors, as well as their family and loved ones.

ATTITUDES TOWARDS DONATION

How people feel about donations and transplants is a very personal issue. Some people believe that donating organs is incredibly noble and generous, while others are less comfortable with the idea. Often these reasons are cultural or religious in nature. Others are fine with donating certain organs, but are uncomfortable with donating others. For example, someone might have no problem donating their liver and kidneys, but the idea of donating their eyes for cornea transplants might make them uneasy. Still others believe that mixing different parts from different people in one body is wrong. At the end of the day, it is an incredibly personal matter. Everyone needs to make up their own mind regarding their own beliefs and how they might affect the lives of others.

Living donors need to be aware that every surgery has risks, and organ donation, while generally safe, could have dangerous effects. For example, if someone wants to donate a kidney, they need to know that if their remaining kidney fails for any reason, they will then need a transplant themselves.

CHAPTER 4
THE TRANSPLANT PROCESS

Before someone actually receives a new organ, a lot of work goes on behind the scenes. Patients need to be evaluated, they must be matched to available organs, and the organs need to be sent to the patients' locations. After the surgery, there is still a process of recovery to go through. Organ transplantation can be a trying process, but one that usually leads to a significant improvement in the patient's quality of life.

THE WAITING LIST

Transplants are often a last resort treatment when other less invasive options have failed. To determine if someone is right for a transplant, they must undergo many tests, both physical and psychological. The physical tests make sure that the patient is ill enough to need a transplant, but healthy enough to recover from the procedure.

NOT ALL THE SAME

DIFFERENT TYPES OF TRANSPLANTS HAVE DIFFERENT NAMES. AN AUTOGRAFT IS WHEN ORGANS OR TISSUE FROM ONE PART OF THE BODY ARE TRANSPLANTED SOMEWHERE ELSE IN OR ON THE SAME BODY. ALLOGRAFTS ARE TRANSPLANTS DONE BETWEEN TWO MEMBERS OF THE SAME SPECIES. A XENOGRAFT IS A TRANSPLANT BETWEEN TWO DIFFERENT SPECIES.

CHOOSING THE RIGHT RECIPIENT

When an organ becomes available in the United States, OPTN creates a master list of the best matches from its database of patients on waiting lists at designated transplant centers. The patient at the top of the list is considered first. If that patient is too far away from the organ or has become too ill for surgery, the next patient on the list will be contacted. This continues until OPTN and the chosen patient's doctors are sure they have a good match.

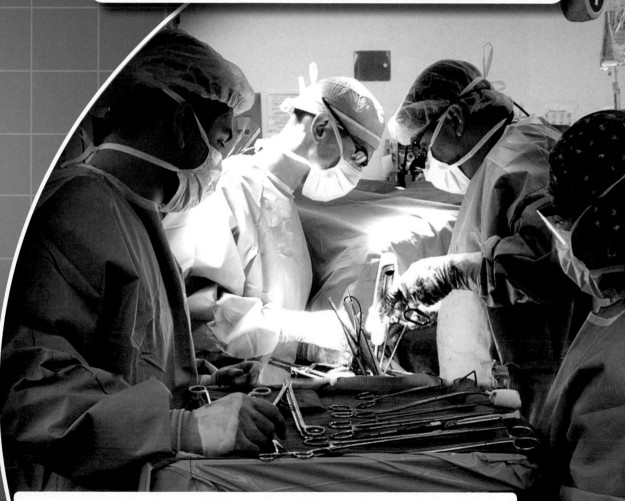

Surgical teams start prepping for transplants the moment they know an organ is on the way. Patients must be alerted to rush to the hospital as well if they are not already at the transplant center. Usually this does not take long, as 75 percent of organs are matched to patients living close by.

Before a patient receives a transplant, they're also checked for conditions that could become more severe following the surgery, like cancer or HIV. They also need to be strong enough to have their immune system suppressed so their body does not reject the organ. Psychological tests make sure that the patient can deal with the stress of the operation and follow their doctor's directions afterwards.

Once they're approved for a transplant, the patient is tested for their blood type, which also helps determine their tissue type. With this information, they're placed on a waiting list for the next available organ that is a good match. OPTN maintains a database with the names of everyone in the country waiting for a kidney, heart, liver, lung, pancreas, intestine, or multiple organs.

Local hospitals inform OPTN when a patient is dying or has died. OPTN then finds out if the person was registered as an organ donor. If they're not, OPTN asks the deceased person's family if they are willing to donate the organs. If they consent, doctors determine which, if any, organs are viable for transplant.

Many states ask people whether they would like to be organ donors when they receive or renew a driver's license. Those under 18 who are getting their license, however, need permission from a parent or guardian to become an organ donor.

Helicopters, planes, and ambulances are used to transport organs as quickly as possible. Large transplant centers often have choppers and planes on standby as well as ambulances.

The length of time a person spends on a waiting list for an organ depends on multiple issues. The rarity of the patient's blood and tissue type is a major one. Often, the rarer the types, the longer the person spends on the list. Some organs are also more widely available than others, such as kidneys. The severity of the patient's condition is also a factor, with the sickest people getting organs first. Distance and time also play a part. If an organ has to travel less distance to get to someone, they have a better chance of getting it. If a person has been on a waiting list for a year, they're more likely to receive an organ than someone who was just placed on the list.

KEEPING THE ORGAN ALIVE

Once an available organ is found, time is of the essence. As soon as an organ is removed, it needs to be prepared for transport. Organs can only be kept healthy outside of the body for a short amount of time, so they need to get where they're going fast.

Different organs are transported differently. Hearts are usually stored on ice in a camping cooler, like the kind you'd use for beverages and food on a family trip. Livers are chilled in saltwater. Kidneys are either shipped with a machine that continually pumps them with preserving fluid, or they're filled with preserving fluid and put on ice. Once the organs are packed, they are shipped using the fastest possible method. They might be driven in a car, or flown in an airplane or helicopter. Since the organ arriving on time is a literal life-or-death matter, it's no surprise they're shipped in a hurry.

RECOVERY

After surgery, patients remain under observation at the hospital. They usually undergo procedures that test how well their new organ is doing. These tests differ based on what organ was replaced. A patient with new lungs might exercise while under observation, while someone with a new heart would receive an **electrocardiogram**. Both would receive chest X-rays. Blood tests are common for all transplant patients, as is a biopsy, where a small amount of the transplanted organ is removed and checked for any evidence of rejection.

After leaving the hospital, the patient will still need to go back for regular check-ups. Immediately after the operation, these might happen a few times a week. However, check-ups will occur less frequently as time goes on and the patient remains well. Often, a once-a-year exam becomes all that's necessary. However, the patient will often remain on immunosuppressive drugs for the rest of their lives.

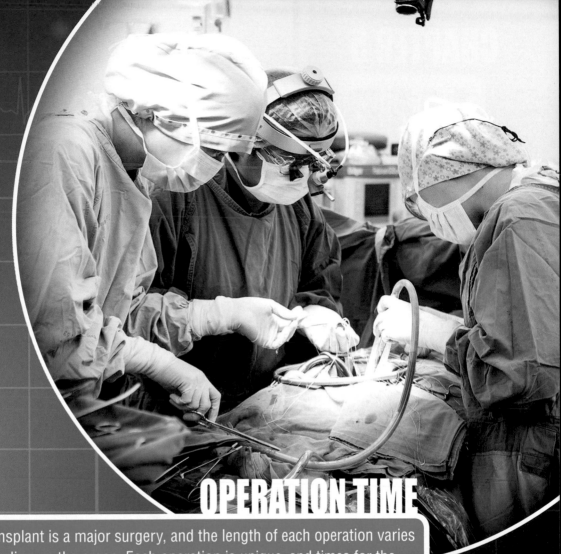

OPERATION TIME

A transplant is a major surgery, and the length of each operation varies depending on the organ. Each operation is unique, and times for the same procedure can differ greatly. Most operations take at least a few hours. Here are some sample times for transplant surgeries:

- Heart   3-4 hours
- Liver   5-8 hours
- Kidney   2-5 hours
- Pancreas   2-4 hours

Procedures involving multiple organs also generally take longer than those involving just one.

CHAPTER 5

IMPROVING SURVIVAL

Once an organ has been successfully transplanted, there are still several steps that must be taken to ensure that the patient survives. The end of the operation is not the end of the organ transplant process. Patients continue to be monitored for the rest of their lives. Although transplantation has become much safer in the last few decades, there are still risks, and these need to be watched for. Both patients and doctors need to be very careful to make sure that successful organ transplants remain successful.

Patients must return to their doctors for regular check-ups and testing that may include tissue sampling and blood tests. Unless the donor was an identical twin, patients must keep taking anti-rejection medication. In either case, they should maintain a healthy weight and avoid smoking and illegal drug use.

Patients will be asked to monitor their own weight, temperature, pulse, and blood pressure at home. Diabetics will need to continue to monitor their blood sugar as well.

BIG DEMAND

THERE ARE MILLIONS OF PEOPLE LIVING WITH TRANSPLANTED ORGANS WORLDWIDE. IN JUST THE UNITED STATES, THERE WERE ALMOST 30,000 PEOPLE WHO RECEIVED A TRANSPLANT IN 2014 ALONE!

CONTACTING A DONOR FAMILY

Although it is sometimes possible for an organ recipient to meet their deceased donor's family, this happens only in about 5 percent of transplants. More often, the recipient will send a thank-you letter to the family through the transplant center without any personal contact. In cases with living donors, the transplant center also can provide continuing health information about the donor without revealing their identity. For many donor families, contact may be too emotionally difficult. Recipients may feel survivor guilt, which is a psychological condition. A recipient may feel guilty for being healthy because of a donor's sacrifice.

When donor families do reach out, they may establish close and satisfying relationships with those who received their loved ones' organs.

IMMUNOSUPPRESSION AND ORGAN REJECTION

The body's immune system is responsible for recognizing and destroying foreign cells that might do the body harm. While this is generally a good thing, in the case of organ transplants, it can be very dangerous. This is because the immune system recognizes that the new organ isn't a natural part of the body, and assumes it shouldn't be there. It then begins trying to fight off the organ's foreign cells. This is called organ rejection. There are two main ways doctors try to stop this from happening. The first is to match the patient's tissue and blood type as closely as possible to the donor organ. The more similar the organ is to the host's original organ, the less likely it is that the immune system will recognize it as foreign. If the immune system doesn't realize that the organ is foreign, it won't try to destroy it.

Blood tests measure a patient's level of immunosuppressive drugs. They also tell doctors whether a patient has normal blood chemistry or may be developing a problem.

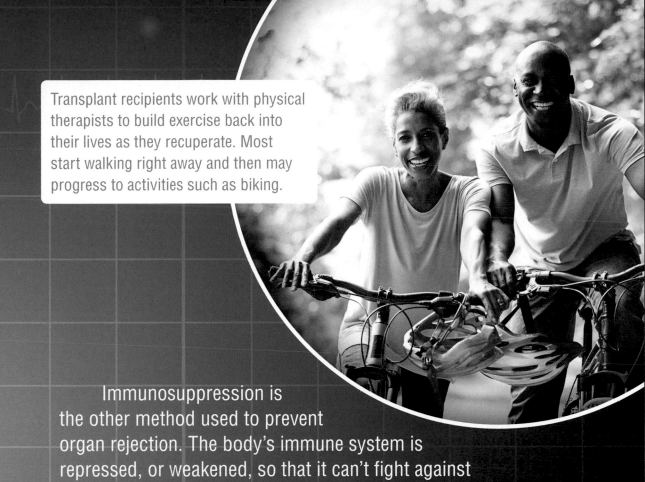

Transplant recipients work with physical therapists to build exercise back into their lives as they recuperate. Most start walking right away and then may progress to activities such as biking.

Immunosuppression is the other method used to prevent organ rejection. The body's immune system is repressed, or weakened, so that it can't fight against the new organ.

When organ transplants were new, radiation treatments were used to achieve this. Eventually, drugs were developed that performed the same function. Some even target specific immune cells, while leaving the rest of the system alone. Today, a patient might receive drugs, radiation therapy, or a combination of the two to ensure that their immune system does not reject their new transplant.

However, there are some risks involved with immunosuppression. Because the immune system is responsible for fighting off infection, suppressing it can make a person more vulnerable to illness.

Under immunosuppression, even a simple cold can develop into a potentially deadly illness if the immune system cannot fight it off. Cancer is also more likely to develop, as the immune system does not recognize and eliminate abnormal cells as it normally would. Both radiation treatments and immunosuppressive drugs can have unpleasant side effects, as well. These might include vomiting, kidney and liver damage, and digestive issues.

SHORTAGE OF ORGANS

In the United States alone there are usually over 100,000 people waiting for a transplant. Every 10 minutes a new person is added to OPTN's waiting list. Although procurement agencies are doing everything they can to secure viable organs and deliver them as quickly as possible, what's really needed is more donors. Many people aren't aware of how to become an organ donor, or that becoming a living donor is possible. As a result, many patients are using new methods to reach out to possible donors. People have begun using social media to try to find someone willing to donate a needed organ. On the upside, advances in medicine mean that more people than ever before are viable donors. This is why education is important to the donation process. If people are aware of what a positive difference they can make in someone's life, they're more likely to become organ donors.

HANDLING MEDICATIONS

Drug therapy has become a key element in the long-term survival of transplant patients. Along with anti-rejection medications, patients often take other drugs, such as steroids, that help the immunosuppressants do their job. They also may continue taking medications to treat the underlying condition that caused them to need a transplant in the first place. Because their immune systems have been weakened, they may need preventative medication at times, as well.

Managing this combination of so many medications can be tricky as doctors continually fine-tune the specific drugs and dosages. A good pharmacist is an important partner for post-transplant patients navigating a changing maze of medications. Pharmacists are trained to know what drugs do, what the side effects are, and when and how they should be taken. Pharmacists double-check patient records to make sure they are not allergic to a prescribed medication and keep an eye out for potentially harmful drug interactions. They also can provide practical tips for storing medicines and setting up reminders for taking each dose.

CHAPTER 6

THE FUTURE OF TRANSPLANT SURGERY

Today, transplant surgery is much more common, and much safer, than it ever has been before. But there's always room for improvement, and doctors and researchers are busy developing new techniques and approaches to transplantation every day.

ROBOTIC SURGERY

Until the 1980s, most major surgeries required a large incision that took weeks to heal, caused significant post-operative pain, and risked serious complications. For example, kidney donors used to expect a large incision and up to a week of recovery time in the hospital. However, recent advances in robotic technology have led to a much less invasive surgical procedure called laparoscopy. Previously, it was believed that removing a kidney was too delicate a procedure to be performed robotically, but this is no longer the case.

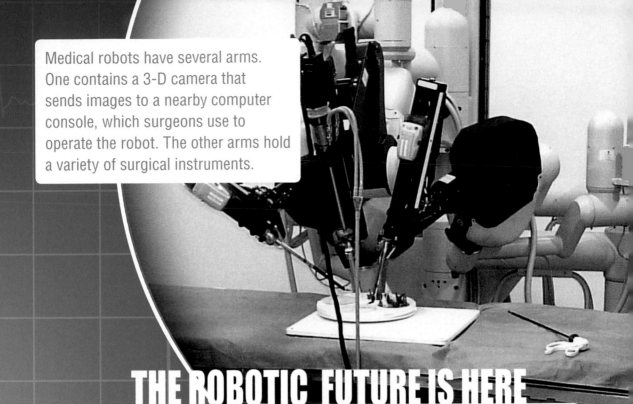

Medical robots have several arms. One contains a 3-D camera that sends images to a nearby computer console, which surgeons use to operate the robot. The other arms hold a variety of surgical instruments.

THE ROBOTIC FUTURE IS HERE

In recent years, new robotic technology has enabled doctors to perform laparoscopic surgery much more precisely. These robots use a 3-D camera and a computer that allows surgeons to control robot arms which can perform very small, fine motions.

Since the late 2000s, robotic surgery has been available for many major operations, including kidney transplants. Someday it may become the standard for transplant operations.

Researchers now are hoping to create miniaturized robot devices so surgeries can become even less invasive and more precise. They are also working on robot-computer combinations that can perform surgery on their own!

With this new technology, a surgeon uses a computer to view the inside of a donor's body. The surgeon is able to use specially designed grips to manipulate small tools that are placed inside the patient. These grips control a robot, which moves the tools.

Laparoscopic technology allows for incredibly precise movements. Because the surgery uses a smaller incision, and is less invasive, post-operative pain is reduced. Recovery time is also much shorter, with some donors leaving the hospital as soon as a day after surgery!

ARTIFICIAL ORGANS

Because there is always a shortage of needed organs, some researchers are working on solutions that remove the need for donors altogether. One branch of research involves developing technology that can perform functions normally done by organs. These human-made devices are called artificial organs.

This isn't a new branch of science. Dialysis machines have existed for decades. They are able to filter the blood of people with faulty or damaged kidneys. However, they're very large machines that a patient often needs to visit the hospital to use. Scientists have been working for years to develop a more portable solution. One recent attempt at a solution uses a device that is combined with a membrane that allows certain substances to pass through it. The device is implanted in the patient's abdomen. It still needs to be connected to a machine located outside of the body to finish the filtration process, though.

Artificial hearts have been in development since at least the 1960s. Although significant advances have been made, current models still need to be hooked up to a large, external power source, making them fairly impractical. Artificial livers, made up of a pump connected to cloned liver cells, are sometimes used in patients who are waiting for a transplant, but they are not a permanent solution. Artificial lungs that use a balloon to imitate the organs' function have also been developed, but, again, are not a permanent solution. As research continues, it's hoped that someday artificial organs will be developed that function more permanently instead of providing a temporary solution for waiting donors.

GROWING NEW ORGANS

Scientists are also investigating the possibility of growing new organs. After all, if you could simply grow an organ whenever someone needed one, a lack of donors wouldn't be such a big problem. Much research is being done into the use of stem cells to grow new organs. Stem cells are a unique kind of cell that have the ability to grow into any kind of cell. Using a patient's own stem cells to grow a replacement organ would solve two of the main issues with current transplants. It would eliminate the need for donors, and it would negate organ rejection. Since the organ would be grown from the patient's own cells, the immune system would not recognize it as foreign and attempt to fight it off. This would also remove the need for immunosuppressive drugs, which can lead to deadly infections.

TIMELINE OF ORGAN TRANSPLANT DEVELOPMENTS

Emerich Ullman successfully transplants a kidney from one dog into the neck of another.

1902

First human-to-human blood transfusion is performed by Dr. James Blundell.

1818

The first living kidney donation is made between identical twins Ronald and Richard Herrick.

1954

ABO blood system is discovered by Karl Landsteiner.

1901

1933

Yurii Voronoy completes the first human-to-human kidney transplant, using an organ from a deceased donor.

Dr. Christiaan Barnard performs the first successful human-to-human heart transplant, with the patient surviving for 18 days after surgery.

1967

1989

First transplant of a small intestine is performed.

1986

The Organ Procurement and Transplantation Network is established in the United States.

2005

The first successful partial face transplant is performed in France.

1980

Cyclosporine, an immunosuppressive drug that helps prevent organ rejection, begins use in treatment.

GLOSSARY

abdomen: The region of the body that houses the digestive organs.

antibody: A protein made by blood that targets and kills antigens.

antigen: A foreign substance that provokes an immune response from the body.

biological: Relating to living organisms.

dialysis: An artificial method of cleansing the blood, developed to replace the function of the kidneys.

electrocardiogram: A medical test that measures the electrical activity in the heart.

immunosuppression: The act of suppressing, or weakening, the immune system so that it does not attack a transplanted organ.

nutrients: The parts of foods that the body uses to grow and stay healthy.

surgery: A method of medical treatment that involves using tools to cut into or otherwise manipulate a patient's body.

transfusion: The process in which blood is taken from one person and put into someone else's body.

viable: Able to be used.

FOR MORE INFORMATION

BOOKS

Foran, Racquel. *Organ Transplants*.
Edina, MN: ABDO Publishing Company, 2014.

Daniels, Patricia and Christina Wilsdon. *Ultimate Bodypedia:
An Amazing Inside-Out Tour of the Human Body*.
Washington, DC: National Geographic Kids, 2014.

Gray, Susan H. *Transplants*.
North Mankato, MN: Cherry Lake Publishing, 2013.

WEBSITES

www.unos.org
United Network for Organ Sharing, USA.

www.innerbody.com
Learn about the human body through interactive anatomy pictures
and descriptions.

INDEX

A

antibodies 5
antigens 5, 9
antiseptics 7, 8
artificial organs 42
autograft 28

B

Barnard, Dr.
 Christiaan 9, 13, 45
blood transfusion(s)
 5, 7, 44
blood types 5
Blundell, Dr. James 7, 44
brain 10, 19, 25
brain dead 13, 25

D

deceased donors 20, 25
dialysis machines 42
digestive system 10, 16
directed donation 22

G

good samaritan donor 21

H

heart 9, 10, 12, 13, 14,
 15, 18, 25, 30, 32,
 33, 45

I

immune system 5, 7, 9,
 13, 30, 36, 37, 38, 43
immunosuppression
 9, 36, 37
immunosuppressive
 drugs 32, 36, 38, 43
insulin 19
intestine 12, 16, 17, 18,
 19, 22, 30, 45

K

kidney(s) 8, 9, 11, 12, 15,
 16, 19, 20, 24, 26, 27, 30,
 31, 32, 33, 38, 40, 41,
 42, 44

L

Landsteiner, Karl 5, 44
Laparoscsopy 40, 41
Lister, Dr. Joseph 8
liver 12, 17, 18, 19, 22,
 27, 30, 33, 38, 43
living donor 20, 26, 38
lungs 12, 14, 15, 20, 25,
 32, 43

O

organ donor 20, 26,
 30, 38
Organ Procurement and
 Transplantation Network
 (OPTN) 11, 29
organ rejection 36
organ trafficking 24

P

pancreas 12, 17, 19,
 22, 30, 33
Pasteur, Louis 8
plastic surgery 4

R

related donors 22
robotic surgery 40, 41

S

skin grafts 4
surgical wounds 8

T

Tagliacozzi, Gaspare 4,
 6, 7

U

Ullman, Emerich 8, 44
United Network for Organ
 Sharing (UNOS) 11

V

Voronoy, Yurii 8, 44

W

waiting list 24, 30, 31, 38

/